Silent Healer

Brittney Perillo

WestBow
PRESS
A DIVISION OF THOMAS NELSON

ISBN: 978-1-4497-6992-5 (e)
ISBN: 978-1-4497-6993-2 (sc)
ISBN: 978-1-4497-6994-9 (hc)

Library of Congress Control Number: 2012918843

WestBow Press books may be ordered through booksellers or by contacting:

WestBow Press
A Division of Thomas Nelson
1663 Liberty Drive
Bloomington, IN 47403
www.westbowpress.com
1-(866) 928-1240

Printed in the United States of America

WestBow Press rev. date: 11/28/2012

Table of Contents

Forward

With a passionate heart for women Brittney displays her desires for us to realize our value in God, seeing ourselves as He sees us. Through this book she boldly outstretches her hand to link with ours to walk through this journey of emotional healing. Her evident hope is that we are able to experience God as an intimate healer and the lover of our soul. She believes that no matter what has happened to you, where you have been, or where you are now, healing in Christ Jesus is available, and you can walk whole in Him for the rest of your life.

Special Dedication and Thanks to....

Special Dedication.......
I want to take the time to dedicate Silent Healer to the four women who wrote their stories of pain and healing for the sections of this book. God has worked in and through all of you to share stories of deep hurt and tragedy to initiate true freedom and healing in others lives. Through all of you, women around the world will be liberated in Christ and heal in totality because of your courage to tell your stories in such a raw vulnerability. Your willingness to be open and available for all to see is encouraging to me and I am forever changed by each of your stories.

You will forever take residence up in my heart for allowing me to share your pain and healing with a hurting, wounded world. Thank you! I love you all.

Thank you.....
My husband Richard, who God has blessed me abundantly with. You are more than I could have ever asked for or imagined in any capacity of a husband and a man. Your strength, courage and unconditional love is breath taking I love you more every day.

My parents, Keith and Barbara Gilliam who God has strategically placed in my life for more reasons than I can count. He redeemed and restored the relationship we have and I am forever grateful. Thank you. I love you both.

My sister, who inspires me to love harder and work harder every day and sacrifice for the children we love the most. You are a courageous woman. I love you.

My family in Buffalo, NY who are forever shaping me into the person I am becoming in Christ. Being around all of you has created stability in an unfamiliar place. You are truly a blessing. I love you all.

To my dear friends whose support and prayers have carried me through every step of this journey with Silent Healer. You continued to lift me up and encourage the God in me even when I had nothing left to give. Thank you.

A thank you to all those who read, proofed and helped with editing of Silent Healer. I appreciate your time and the extending of your talents and gifts to help my words make sense to others.

And thank you to God. Without You none of this would ever be possible. You have shown me your glory in ways unimaginable. You have redeemed me, restored me, and rescued me. I wake up every morning thankful that you chose me, I did not choose you. You loved me before I ever loved you. I have no words that could describe who you are to me. You are my everything and I thank you for giving me the opportunity to know what that means in my every day life. I am yours and I cannot wait to see what you will do in the time to come. All the praise, honor and glory goes to you forever and ever. I love you!

Preface

Silent Healer was written with hurting, wounded, broken women in mind. If we can be honest with ourselves, we all relate to this statement in some manner. We all have mending, forgiving, letting go and healing to do in some shape, form or fashion.

A friend of mine once said, "I am in so much pain, but God is so silent." Without hesitation I responded, "In the greatest silence Jesus Christ ever knew from God, He died on a cross and everything changed. God changed the whole world in that silence." I have experienced pain greater than I thought I could endure, along with emotions that I thought I was never capable of bearing. God's silence in those times was very troubling to me. What I did not realize at the time was God's silence was part of a process in order for Him to change my life to fulfill His purpose in my life.

Regardless of my experiences, and the toll it has taken, I believe our healing is based on our willingness to hear God in the silence of our wounded hearts and allow him to meet us in our despair. His desire for us is to begin living our lives abundantly in Him. We can only do that completely, when we allow Him to gently care for our hearts through His Word and Spirit.

"My soul, wait silently for God alone, for my expectation *is* from Him. He only *is* my rock and my salvation; *He is* my defense; I shall not be moved. In God *is* my salvation and my glory; The rock of my strength, *And* my refuge, *is* in God. Trust in Him at all times, you people; Pour out your heart before Him; God *is* a refuge for us." (Psalm 62:5-8 NKJV)

Come join me as we embark on a journey of true healing, freedom, and wholeness in God.

Introduction

I am so excited you have decided to embark on a spiritual healing process with God. I look forward to what God is going to do in and through you as you experience Him through this book.

I'd like to begin with a story of a man named Job from the Bible. I really like Job because he is a prime example of someone who endured many painful situations in his life and instead of denying God, he held onto his hope in God and believed he would one day be delivered from the pain and be healed.

Job is a man who had everything and everyone he needed in his life. He had a relationship with God and was very faithful in all that he did. One day Satan saw Job and asked God's permission to sift him. Satan believed that he could get Job to curse God through great pain and trials. With God's permission, Satan's request was granted.

Satan began causing Job physical, emotional, and mental pain. He lost everything God had given him. He lost his family to death, friends by betrayal, and possessions by destruction. As Job continued to endure the greatest pain he had ever known, he begged God for healing. Much to his surprise, while in agony, God was silent.

Job experienced God's silence for 37 chapters in the Bible. Can you imagine that there are 42 chapters in the book of Job and for 37 of them God was silent? Clearly, God is making a point to His children about who He is, even when we suffer great heartache.

Job prayed and begged in desperation for God. The primary focus of the story is him yearning for God to stop the pain.

I am brought to my knees as a reader on behalf of Job pleading with God to deliver him. I can feel his agony. I can empathize with him and it is painful to hear the way he describes his hurt. Not only was God silent, but Job was suffering the worst pain of his life.

How can this happen? Job needed God to speak hope into his life and He was totally silent. The only hope that Job could hold onto was what he knew to be true about God. In fact during one of his desperate prayers to God he said:

"For I know that my Redeemer lives, and He shall stand at last on the earth; and after my skin is destroyed, this I know, that in my flesh I shall see God, whom I shall see for myself, and my eyes shall behold, and not another. How my heart yearns within me!" (Job 19: 25-27 NKJV)

Job knew God before all of his tragedies and he had to believe God for who He said He was before the pain began. His prayer did not remove his agony; rather his belief and faith in a healing God helped him carry on. Job believed that if God heard and loved him before his life was in shambles, surely then, God would not change when his pain increased and his flesh doubted the goodness of God. Finally, God broke His silence. Not only did God speak, but eventually He intervened and delivered Job from his afflictions, restoring his life more abundantly than before the wounds emerged. Job had unshakeable faith in God even in the midst of sorrow and God's silence. He couldn't make sense of his tragedies, but he still believed God for his redemption and healing.

What if we could all take a page from Job's book, both

literally and figuratively? What if believing that God is our healer and redeemer in the midst of the darkest silence of our soul, is what it would take to eventually hear Him? Allowing God to meet us in those most painful places of our lives and inviting Him to enter even when we cannot imagine how He could begin to heal us. We don't have to know how He will; we just have to believe He will.

This healing journey will be challenging. We must allow God to meet us in places of great loss, deep wounds, horrific pain, and bitter hopelessness. The focus will be centered on God meeting us in the silent places of our souls, where only you and He know the pain that exists.

I am excited to take this journey of healing together, in faith, that you will experience freedom and hope in Christ. We will look at women in today's society, as well as women in the Bible and their stories to guide us on an intimate path to healing, redemption and restoration. I pray you will allow God to change your life through His word and by His love.

Chapter 1
The Deep Collide

When I think of the word, "collide", it's unsettling. I think of a conflict. A conflict requires taking care of a problem with a solution. With an effective solution we can avoid revisiting the issue again. In this chapter, I want to discuss the spiritual aspect of the conflict we are faced with when the reality of our pain collides with the ability we have to heal in Christ. Our natural reaction to pain and brokenness could be to hold it deep within ourselves. Our human nature may often be to run from deep wounds. Wounds that need to be taken care of and dealt with in order for us to heal; but healing challenges us to face reality, even though our reality seems simply too hard to face. I would, however, consider confronting the pain to be a breaking point in our spiritual growth. True brokenness can only breed wholeness if healed by God. Our ultimate desire, as Christians, is to be whole in Him. We have free will, and this conflict leaves us with a decision to make.

A love.....

My freshman year of college was a year to remember. I

was 18, out of my house for the first time and I was making my own life about an hour away from home. I was young, immature and did not really care much about the educational aspect of college, but more the social. I really disliked high school and was never someone to hang out with anyone from school outside the walls of the building it was held in. I was more into church and my youth group friends. So when I got to college, something happened, something sparked, this was my chance to be the social butterfly I had always wanted to be. Perhaps it was the Christian college that made me feel so much like myself or it could have been that I finally realized the importance of getting out of my comfort zone and meeting new people. Either way, I loved my new found freedom. Spiritually I was more excited than I had ever been about God and who He was in my life. My faith was becoming my own and I was surrounded by people that felt the same.

Half way through my freshman year I met a strikingly handsome young man, we will call him David. He was an athlete, charming, funny, smart and he was a Christian. I was falling for him and I found myself enticed by his very presence in my life, just being around him was enough to give me butterflies and loss of words. He was perfect for me, or so I thought. He had all the right things a girl looks for in a man. But the one thing he didn't have was the stamp of approval from my parents, so of course I broke it off immediately. Disobeying them was not an option, I loved them too much.

At the time, I could not make sense in my own mind as to why my parents disliked this relationship so much and it hurt, but I had to accept it. I would cry out and beg God for an answer, begging him to intervene on my behalf and tell them the relationship was suitable. Nothing gave, and I was miserable.

Fall semester of my sophomore year I took it upon myself to start dating David again and went against everything my parents had said. This time I went two feet in never looking back. I had fallen in love with this man, and no one could tell me different. I was the happiest girl in the world at school, but when I would go home to visit I was holding in a secret that was eating me alive. That Christmas break, I came clean about David and the relationship I was in to my parents, willing to take the punishment at any cost, even if that cost meant losing them.

I could not make sense of my thoughts at the time. I was 20 years old, unwavering stubbornly on an issue that I could never change, no matter how hard I fought, and I knew that. If someone would have asked me then, I would have told them that I thought I could change the world with this one stand. I thought for sure God would send a ripple effect across the world, changing the hearts of millions to line up with my position on this issue. Sometimes being 20 and disillusioned is all the excuse we need for our actions, agreed?

Looking back, I know that the way I went about these things was wrong, but I was bound and determined to prove my point, even if how I handled it was not the most honoring of ways.

I explained to my parents that I did not agree with them about David. I wanted a relationship with them and him as well, but wasn't allowed to have both. As all three of us sat there devastated for the same reasons, none of which we would care to admit. We knew that everything we had known about our relationship was about to change for the worst.

This began the hardest three years of my life to this date. I had lost everything in an instant. I was deeply rooted in my fear of losing the love of my life or the parents I loved and cared for so deeply.

David became my world because he was all that was left of it. Everything I knew for 20 years of my life had vanished and he was all I knew or wanted to know.

I began to blame God for my wretched pain and loneliness. I would shout at him that He could fix it, but wouldn't. I cried at the drop of a hat and argued with David more every day because of the hurt inside. I would beat him up verbally then beg for him not to leave me. Looking back, I was reacting out of a wounded heart and saw him as a source of great pain, but the thought of losing him was unbearable. The enemy would feed me lies that God was not interested in my heartache and I was slipping down a downward spiral that felt like a living hell in my soul. I couldn't feel anything without it being accompanied by anger and bitterness.

People kept feeding me lies, bathing it in concern that everything would work out, eventually. They thought this was encouragement, but to me, it was a reminder of the harsh reality that my heart was divided. Things were not working out at all and at the end of every day, I would lay my head on my pillow at night dreading waking up the next day only to face the destructive behavior and empty life I had come to know.

I eventually stopped asking God to fix it and started drinking and partying to numb it. I was alone, angry, hurt and no one understood because the two people that knew me best, my parents, were not even on speaking terms with me. I would long for the weekends, just so I could forget the moments that had pierced me the most from that week. Every wound was getting deeper and the tape deck in my head kept rewinding the painful scenes in my mind that kept me in the rut I had come to be comforted by.

For a year, I would go back and forth with God, myself and the enemy and I would believe every lie the enemy fed to me about who I was and I would know God thought different, but I did not have the strength to fight it. The enemy had convinced me that this was all worth it as long as I had David. I had lost myself in a relationship that I allowed to define every aspect of my life, including my walk with God. I found myself becoming someone I did not recognize in the mirror. The relationship had started out with pure intentions, but quickly turned into one that consumed me in an unhealthy manner.

I believed I could not live life without this man; I couldn't manage at all. We had several break ups and then we would get back together. Without consulting God at all, I would enter back into this relationship every time because I couldn't bear the thought of facing the devastation of the break-up. I was disobedient when God told me to let it go. I was defining myself by a relationship that was poison for the both of us. I did not want to face losing him because I had lost everyone else in the midst of all my choices. I was fading, but still standing by the choice I had made to follow through with this relationship. Everything inside of me told me that I was standing my ground and making a point. I believed with all my heart that if I could make this relationship work with David that my parents would have a change of heart. I was determined to be the one who changed them, but I could not and it was not my place to take on that responsibility. I held on to a relationship to prove a point. I wanted to know that the decision I made was not going to be wasted but worth it in the end. It wasn't!

One night while sitting in a parking lot, in his car, David broke up with me. The world I had known for two years and fought bitterly for came to a halting end. Sitting there that night I felt a peace, but not one that I was willing to acknowledge at the time. He was doing something that I myself would never have the strength to do, but knew it needed to be done. I was in shock and disbelief that he had just broken up with me for the final time. I was searching for answers and asking a lot of questions, holding back tears while dying inside. I could not speak. It was over, and I could not save it with anything. I got out of the car that night and drove home in complete horror. Everything I had given up for this relationship was gone, and so was David. I was lost.

Reality Check

At this point David and I had been broken up for roughly a year, but of course stayed in contact for no healthy reason that I could conjure up. Am I the only one who has fallen for this situation after a break-up? I still loved him and did not know how to fully walk away from him, even as a friend.

I was in the very preliminary stages of really learning how to heal in God and getting to know God deeper. I was making head way and was sure I was on the fast track to recovery for the wounded, broken and destroyed. Also to mention, I was positive once I got back on the right track with God that He would, of course, put David and I back together. So I was ready to get to my 'Happily ever after ending, with a little detour, but it all worked out' stage. Right? After all, getting back together with David was obviously one of my heart's desires and God gives us those, correct? I could not see why He wouldn't! Why wouldn't God want this for me? It was all that made sense to me. Do you ever notice that when we want something, so saturated in our own selfish desires, that we cannot even imagine what life would be like if we did not get them? We cannot seem to imagine them not being what God wants for us as well. This makes me wonder how many times we should question if 'our' heart's desires are even worthy of the fraction of the heart we have invested into them. That was David for me. Have you been there? With that said, I was not ready for what happened next.

David and I constantly had these seasons of deciding not to talk, but of course I could not oblige and ended up calling him and I would be emotionally reeled back in. This was one of those calls, we had not talked in months and I missed him and just wanted to hear his voice. At times, I tend to be a stubborn person and even though God said "no" to my great idea of calling him this night, I still did. I called and he answered. It was in that very moment my entire world collapsed. It was then that all of the hurt that I had been afraid of for so long in this situation collided with the healing God intended for my life. I didn't realize it then, but I was at my breaking point of healing, and I, too, had a decision to make.

David was unemotionally involved in the conversation and clearly had no intentions of ever getting back together. Too much time had passed and life had gone on. I could tell he was removed because of his interest in other things that did not involve me, one of which I could tell was another girl. He had a clear disinterest in me or anything I had to say. The very scene I was afraid of was unfolding on the other side of the phone. He had moved on with his life and I was not in it and worse he did not want me in it. I acted unaffected, said good-bye and hung up quickly!

Inside my head were the thoughts and questions: How could he be so cold? I needed him!! I wanted him! I couldn't move on without him in my life! Did he not understand? Did he not care about the pain I was in? Why doesn't this hurt him? How could he have let go so easily?

I was rooted and driven by every wrong thing and knew it. My questions and thoughts revealed the level of insecurity in my heart about who I really was without this man. I was disgusted with myself and my reactions and I knew the only way out was with God. My heart was truly sick and Gods healing was the remedy I needed.

The hope that I had held on to for so long, that after our break-up we would still have a chance to be together, was shattered that night in about five minutes.

Isn't it ironic, that in life, we have a tendency to hold on to some things with a tight grip, for years, that when they finally slip between our fingers it can take a simple insignificant phone conversation for it to be completely snatched out of our grasp?!

I had invested so much of my heart and I wasn't ready to give up yet. As I sat on the floor of that quiet room, I knew what I had to do. I knew after all of my fighting, endless tears, and countless prayers, what I dreaded most was inevitably about to happen. The image of the death of this relationship was ugly. I felt the blood rush to my face and I began to sob. I could not breathe for a minute. I used to think people that reacted like this to pain were exaggerating, until I had actually experienced it. It was a pain so deep and piercing that it literally took the breath out of my lungs. I had lost grip of the last strand that I thought held us together.

All of my ideas, dreams, and desires for us, had officially come to an end. After a long hard battle, I had lost the fight for him. I had lost total control of this situation and it deeply hurt. This man had stopped loving, caring, and entertaining any thought of me while he was still my every thought, deepest care, and strongest love. How could this have happened?

I began frantically thinking about how to get him back again, exhausting every idea or sentence I could say in order for him to acknowledge his love for me. I was devastated and all alone. Almost three years of my life was gone in an instant and a person that I loved so much would never love me back. Nothing I could say or do would change the circumstance.

God was so gentle with me that night. He just held me as I cried. I distinctly remember thinking, "What now?" "How can I manage to get up from here?" I wish I could say at this moment that I got up, dusted myself off, and moved on with my life, but that is quite the contrary to what took place in the next year.

I was constantly frazzled in thought and alone, screaming inside for a way out of all my pain. I did not listen to God when He gave me an open door to walk away from consistent sources of destruction in my life. I was hurting and suffering from too many wounds to list, as well as, many people I loved and cared for that contributed to those wounds. I had no idea how I would survive if I let go and let God work in every intricate detail of my broken heart. I knew that I would have to face all of the wounds that had been corrupting my heart for years. This relationship had given me the opportunity to postpone the reality of pain that was stirring in the depths of my soul that needed healing.

I fed myself many lies. I honestly had no idea I could ever move past the pain. Quite frankly, I was scared to do so. I was oblivious to the affect it was having in every other area of my life.

Sometimes, our wounds have been with us for so long, that they become what we hide behind, what we find our value in, and what we find comfort in because it is all that we know. This is a lie and we have to stop believing it.

At the end of this day, all I had was God. The conflict I was faced with was to stay hurt and wounded, or allow God to be the solution to a problem that I would never have to revisit again.

I had a decision to make and so do you. We can truly heal in God and never have to visit the pain of the experience again. He gives us this choice. It may cause pain while we go through it, but wouldn't it be best for us to hurt for a short time rather than infiltrate our hearts negatively for the rest of our lives?

I am not writing this book to compare my wounds with yours or vice versa. I am the first to say that wounds are different in their cause and their severity. This book was not written to say that I have gone through all the possible deep pains every woman ever has or will, but instead my heart is to relate to you. I want to relate to you on a level that pain hurts regardless of what caused it. These things look different on every person, but we are here to get to our healer together.

The sources of the wounds are not what we are here seeking, but rather the source where wounds can find healing. The point of this journey is to give you the option to heal with a

God who is patiently waiting for you to allow Him to work in your life.

Whatever has happened to you has most definitely wounded you or you would not have chosen a book like this to read. Let's look to God for restoration and true healing. If you commit to reading it, you will discover other stories in this book from real women, just like you, that you may relate to as well. Continuing with me will require the acknowledgement of pain, walking through it, grieving, forgiving the ones who hurt, abused, and offended you. Healing requires a heart of endurance, especially when the painful memories are too much to handle and the strength you thought you had weakens. Remember that God is your strength! His grace is all you need.

"Each time he said, "My grace is all you need. My power works best in weakness." So now I am glad to boast about my weaknesses, so that the power of Christ can work through me." (2 Corinthians 12:9 NLT) The verse goes on to say "We are glad whenever we are weak but you are strong" in 2 Corinthians 13:9. (NKJV)

Paul recognizes this concept and we must as well. We will come to know the strength of God and His power in our weaknesses intimately in our time together.

I pray that as you read this book you can understand that any sentence or word that I say will not be the instant 'fix-all" that you are looking for in such a painful place. My hope is that you will understand the only reason I can even write this book is because the One who healed me, can heal you.

You must know that there is life after hurt and pain. There is a God who loves and cares for you deeply, and I pray that our time together will be a starting point for your healing. I pray that this book will be a tool God uses to reveal Himself to you.

I know it will be difficult at the beginning, but I want to encourage you to hold on and push through every emotion inside of you that may cause you to run in another direction.

Remember:

Conflict requires taking care of a problem with a solution. With an effective solution it will avoid revisiting the issue again.

After this chapter, take a moment to prepare your heart and mind for what God desires for you at this appointed time in your healing process.

Chapter 2
Shattered

"Going through the motions doesn't please you; a flawless performance is nothing to you. I learned God-worship when my pride was shattered. Heart-shattered lives ready for love don't for a moment escape God's notice."
Psalm 51:16-17
(The Message)

"Shattered." This used to be the word that I used to describe, on a daily basis; for how I felt toward God and the way that healing was taking place in my life. I would tell people that my life was "shattered" or that "my life was in pieces."

Most days, I felt as if I were picking up broken, shattered pieces of a life that used to mean everything to me. I thought of sitting in a room with glass walls. Every wall showed me a part of my life that defined who I was and described where I was headed. Then, all of a sudden someone threw a boulder and every piece of glass shattered onto the floor. Nothing was making sense in every part of my life. Do you relate?

How do we sit there and watch all that we have known, or know, fall apart before us and not have the ability to stop it?

Many women I have talked with can relate to this very experience with a divorce, a loss of a career, physical or sexual abuse. These shattered pieces I referred to can also be described as brokenness in our lives. Often; we can mistake brokenness for a negative connotation. These types of experiences women have gone through such as those stated above, are often the situations that brought them to their knees before God. They came truly broken before Him in need of a healing and love that only He can provide. Brokenness is never wanted, nor desired in any of us. No matter what we experience, God is always there to pick us up. If we have been wounded the only way through it is with God.

When we are wounded it may be easier for us to ask God why, or even tell Him what He should have done for us in the midst of the painful situation. I urge you to not allow yourself to go there as it will hinder your spiritual growth. We must remember God remains the same and is God no matter what obstacle we encounter as He stated in His Word in Hebrews 13:8, "Jesus Christ is the same, yesterday, today, and forevermore." Good people have negative experiences. We can ask many justifying questions, but we will still end up in the same place we were when we began.

When I was going through my own healing journey, I remembered a scene in the movie of *The Passion of the Christ*. It was the part when the viewer sees Jesus' sandal in the sand and a woman clinging to His feet. This scene refers to the woman in the Bible caught in the act of adultery. In John, chapter 8, the Pharisees bring her to Jesus in hopes that He will command them to stone her to death for her actions. She begs for mercy because she knows the consequences of her behavior. Much to their surprise He finds no fault in her.

He picks her up, looks her in the eyes and says, "Go and sin no more."

I love this story because it is a beautiful picture of God's amazing grace and love for His children. I always imagined that God found me this way. For a long time, I had been running from wounds. When God finally got me to my knees, I truly felt I was in this woman's position. Face down on the ground, dirty, hurting, confused, broken, and wounded. All I could do was lay at the feet of the only one who could save me. Can you relate to this woman as well?

Do I really surrender all?

I grew up in church, therefore; the idea of surrendering all of myself to Jesus in the middle of my prodigal days was not how I envisioned my life. I never thought I would run away from God in any capacity, especially when pain came.

I gave my life to Jesus Christ at 16, but at 21, I ran, and I ran hard. Not looking back for a second. I still went to church, and I still wanted God, but I also wanted the heartache to stop. I wanted to feel normal again. For a while, running was what seemed to numb the pain. I wanted more than anything to make things right with my family, friends, and God, but the only way to all of that was walking through the pain that brought me there. I had to walk through my decisions and the consequences that accompanied them, taking responsibility for my own actions and forgive myself. I knew I had to face deep wounds in my heart. This meant forgiving those who hurt me and continuing to love them without holding onto resentment. All of these things seemed impossible to do at the time.

I was chasing a dream that one day it would all go away and things would be normal again. I assumed because I loved God and He loved me that healing would come all on its own and forgiveness would happen overnight. I looked at what the shattered pieces my life had become and all I could do was run more. God made it clear, in order for me to get to the other side of pain; I must walk through the things that hurt the most and allow Him to redeem the feelings that resulted from my wounds. He not only needed to heal me from the hurt, but He needed to redeem my life I had lost due to the hurt. This idea of allowing God to redeem the moments that caused us hurt is something we will look deeper into in a later chapter.

One day I had an epiphany that if I want to heal from things then I have to deal with them. To me that was just one more reason to run. I remember thinking, "God, there is no way I can give you all of this." As I began the process, I realized that He is a patient God and He just wanted it piece by piece. When we think about surrendering everything to God, we often think of literally grabbing every wound, hurt, offense and sin, and handing it to Him.

My suggestion would be to surrender your heart and gently surrender your deep wounds. If you submit them to Him all at once, you may feel overwhelmed and run in the other direction. I know I did.

I would love to say that I woke up one day, feeling particularly ready to give everything to God; but this is nothing but farther from the truth. Healing is a process, and this is why I am calling it a gentle surrender. It seemed right when I would think I was getting somewhere, another piercing level of pain would present itself and I would have to keep giving every part of it to God. I want you to consider surrendering all your wounds to God, but I want you to consider giving them to Him one wound at a time. I do not want you to get overwhelmed. God knows us and I am certain that is not His desire for you either. 1 Peter 5:7 says, "Give all your worries and cares to God, for he cares about you." (NLT)

This verse tells us He cares about all that we carry and He doesn't want us to get overwhelmed by the heaviness of our pain. I want you to look at your shattered glass walls. Examine the specific situations that shattered them to pieces. Imagine the person that hurt you or inflicted pain of any kind on you. Take a minute to be willing to give God one piece at a time. Ponder on these verses out of Psalm 139 as you imagine your life unfolding and the pain you have endured.

"You have searched me, Lord, and you know me. You know when I sit and when I rise; you perceive my thoughts from afar. You discern my going out and my lying down; you are familiar with all my ways. Before a word is on my tongue you, Lord, know it completely. You hem me in behind and before, and you lay your hand upon me. Such knowledge is too wonderful for me, too lofty for me to attain. Where can I go from your Spirit? Where can I flee from your presence? If I go up to the heavens, you are there; if I make my bed in the depths, you are there. If I rise on the wings of the dawn, if I settle on the far side of the sea, even there your hand will guide me, your right hand will hold me fast. If I say, "Surely the darkness will hide me and the light become night around me, even the darkness will not be dark to you; the night will shine like the day, for darkness is as light to you." (Psalm 139:1-12 NIV)

God knows you and He is everywhere you are. You cannot

escape His love and His desire for you to heal. He has known you from the beginning of time and is waiting for you to surrender all your brokenness to Him. I am asking you to consider picking up one broken piece at a time in your life and giving that one piece to God in full surrender.

The first step could be acknowledging that you have been hurt and no matter how big or how small it was, it has deeply affected you. Maybe you have never admitted that a certain situation hurt you and need to be honest with God about it. Scream, shout, cry or whatever you need to do to get it out in the open to Him. Letting God walk us through our true feelings really helps us figure out the real reason we are so hurt. He then teaches us how to heal from that hurt.

God spoke something to my heart one day that said "You have to acknowledge the hurt before you can obtain the healing." I love this! It is so true. Some of us are still waiting to heal after things that have happened long ago because we are in denial and have never admitted that they hurt. How can we know we need God to heal us if we cannot even admit the experience happened, much less that it was hurtful? Some of us have buried wounds so deep that to acknowledge them may be terrifying.

I have to share a story with you from a life of a woman named Tracy. I met her on my journey of writing this book and through a simple conversation, God made it clear to me that she was supposed to share her story with all of you.

I was 5 or 6 years old, a normal loving, playful, and cheerful child. I was innocent and didn't know the dangers lurking before me. Innocence lost and taken all because of a man who desired to put his hands sexually on a little child, and that little child was me.

Why did this happen? Why did he touch me like this? How could he pleasure himself and get enjoyment out of touching a little girl? Why did he have to take it upon himself to take something that was so precious away from me? He took my innocence, childhood, and feelings of being safe and secure. This was our secret, our dirty little secret.

Was it something I did or said to make him think that it was ok to touch me? Did I wear the wrong thing or did I look at him the wrong way? No, this was not my father, but a man who stood in as my father when he married my mother. He chastised and disciplined me while all the time molesting me, touching me in ways that no adult should ever touch a child.

I was confused, hurt, and scared. I dare not tell my mother as I would never want to hurt her. I couldn't let this dirty little secret destroy her life, so I carried it with me, alone and scared.

I told no one, not one soul. Age six turned into seven, seven into eight, eight into nine, nine into ten, ten into eleven, eleven into twelve, twelve into thirteen, thirteen into fourteen. All those years were taken from me. I had no say so on whether I wanted to be touched or not. As a matter of fact, sometimes if I wanted to eat I had a choice, if you let me do this then you can eat.

How does a child make the decision of being hungry or allowing a man to touch her so she can eat? How could an adult, a so called human being put a child in a situation to where she has to choose him for food or remain hungry? How do you get through all those years of keeping this dirty little secret, feeling alone, scared, and hurt?

Well, I got through with the help of God. See, I was born into church. Being raised by my mom and going to church under the leadership of my grandmother who was the Pastor, I found out about God very early in my life. As I got older and heard people talk about what God did for them, I begin to think if God delivered them out of their situation, then maybe, just maybe, he can deliver me out of mine.

I was 14 years old when I called on God one night. I was at the lowest point and I just knew I couldn't take another encounter with this man. I felt I had suffered enough. I felt like I was violated enough and I wanted my body back. I asked God to help me, and I prayed an earnest prayer. I let God know all the emotions and hurt I was feeling. I told God that if he didn't intervene on my behalf I wouldn't make it. I laid in bed and cried and prayed until I feel asleep. Before I knew it, this man was completely out of my life. The night I prayed was the last time he ever touched me. God had heard my cry and I found out at age 14 how real God truly is.

I continued to keep this dirty little secret for the next 4 years as I was very ashamed. I didn't want anyone to know that I had been touched as a child by an adult. What would people think of me? Would they say it was my fault, would they say I was being fast and I should have worn different clothes around him? Would they call me a liar and tell me I just made it all up?

I didn't know, so it was easier to hold this in, so I thought. What I didn't realize was that by holding it in, I was holding on to the hurt, shame, embarrassment, feelings of insecurity, and blame. By not telling I was still giving this man the same power he had when he was molesting me. Now that I had my body back, I needed to take my power back. I told my story to someone very close to me who convinced me to share my story with my mom. I wasn't called a liar, I wasn't told that I was dirty, I wasn't blamed for it and most of all, I was still loved. Yes, I was still loved by my loved ones, but most importantly, I was still loved by God.

You know, sometimes I felt God loved me a little extra just because of the innocence I had lost. God let me know that it wasn't my fault and I can choose to be a survivor in my adult life. I didn't have a choice as a child, but God showed me that as an adult I can choose to live or to continue to be bound by what happened to me as a child. I decided to choose life. I choose to not let that molester have any more power over me, my body, or my life.

There's a congregational song with lyrics that say" look to Jesus now and live", which is what I did. I took my eyes off of my molestation, and I put my eyes on God the deliverer, from the molestation.

I've been healed at different levels of my hurt. Because I suffered for so many years, there were so many roots that sprouted and developed and God has been working on them one by one. The key thing is allowing God to work and being open to God so that you can continually be healed from your past.

The enemy wanted me to believe that I was nothing because of my childhood, and that I couldn't overcome, but the devil was and is a liar. I have overcome and I will continue to overcome the challenges I face as a result of the molestation that happened to me.

Writing my testimony for this book was a challenge, but if you're reading this then you know, God helped me to overcome it! At times I still struggle to talk about the molestation because, in doing so, you have to go back and think about what you've been through. I'm learning now that even in that, God is getting the glory because I can't tell the story without telling the testimony of how God delivered me and is continually restoring me. My testimony represents victory because I was able to overcome the molestation, and the feelings of hurt, embarrassment, feeling dirty & nasty, and being scared and alone. God has let me know that there is no shame and to hold my head high as his child because he has always and will continue to carry me through.

My prayers are that if you are reading this and have been through or currently going through molestation, you will know that it is not your fault. I pray that you can gather enough strength to tell somebody. If you have told somebody, I pray that you have support. Whether a family member, friend, or even a crisis center, there is somebody you can talk to that can help you through this. I pray that the enemy will not let you use this unfortunate circumstance in your life to turn to drugs and alcohol, become promiscuous, or have you do anything out of the will of God to cause harm to your body, mind, or spirit. For it is God's desire that we live and not die.

If God can deliver me, He can and He will do the same for you. You can survive, you will survive. You can live and not die. In Jesus name Amen!

This is a powerful testimony of what God can do, will do, and has done in this woman's life. I have to tell you the reason I am so taken back every time I read it is because she explains how deep she had buried her wounds. She had wounds that God had to heal in order for her to walk in complete freedom in Him. She was still that little girl inside, screaming for help, and a way out of her pain, even when she was a grown woman. She had a choice to make. She could have stayed in a place of anger and bitterness toward her abuser and being honest about this situation, none of us would blame her one bit. Instead, she decided to let God down in the secret place of her soul where only she and God knew the pain and the depth of her wounds. She decided to walk through this pain one shattered piece at a time. It took a lot, and I am sure if you ask her today she would tell you that one of the hardest parts was walking back through the memories and moments that violated her most, but she did it. Not because she wanted to, but because she knew the only way to heal from it, was to deal with it.

Something she said struck me, *"Now that I had my body back, I needed to take my power back."* God not only wants to heal you, but He wants to restore your innocence, time, identity, dignity, self-worth, mind, or anything that you feel has been taken. What was taken from you? How do you get it back? God not only wants to meet you in the middle of your nightmare, but He wants to redeem what has kept you bound. You are valuable and God loves when you and I not only surrender the pain, hurt, and wounds one at a time, but He loves when we allow Him to restore us.

For Tracy, her body and mind were restored. God not only wanted to heal her, but He wanted her to have her body back and have the power to determine what happens with it on her own terms in His name. She is a prime example of gently surrendering your wounds to God one piece at a time.

You are OFF DUTY!

Surrendering your life can begin now, and will involve letting go of the control that the pain has on you, as it did with Tracy. Once someone told me 'God guards your heart, you are off duty.' At the time, I was in a very defensive place with my heart, but that statement gave me a surge of strength to fully surrender the pain that was controlling me.

Give God the control of your heart and allow Him to come in and mend your wounds. Allow God to speak to you about whether or not you are still trying to guard your own heart from even Him. God knows the reason you are guarded is to keep people from the deep places that hurt you most. He is the only one who is going with you on this journey. You don't have to share your shattered pieces with anyone besides Him. Your safe place is with Him. He has made you and He wants to go to the depths with you so you can become all that He desires for you to be. He can redeem your life, heal your wounds, grow your heart, and teach you about Himself and His true love for you every step of the way.

Chapter 3
The Power of a Whisper

"Then he was told, "Go, stand on the mountain at attention before God. God will pass by." A hurricane wind ripped through the mountains and shattered the rocks before God, but God wasn't to be found in the wind; after the wind an earthquake, but God wasn't in the earthquake; and after the earthquake fire, but God wasn't in the fire; and after the fire a gentle and quiet whisper. When Elijah heard the quiet voice, he muffled his face..." 1 Kings 19:11-14a (The Message)

In 1 Kings 19:11-14, Elijah was listening for God and he was listening in all the ways he thought God would speak to him, in wind, earthquake, and fire. In comparison, we may think God will speak loudly and abruptly in the midst of our pain in order for us to know He is there. Instead, Elijah heard nothing until the storms had passed and the damage was done. It was then that he heard God's whisper.

What if this is the moment we are waiting for in our own lives? This chapter is about God whispering in the midst of a painful place.

When God began to whisper in the midst of my wounds, I ignored him. I thought, "Well, if He is not willing to say it louder, then I'm not willing to listen." I had convinced myself that the whisper was God's disinterest in me and that God was far from the pain.

As I began to explore the idea of God whispering to me in the depth of my pain, I found a very interesting definition of the word whisper, "A low, soft, sibilant voice or utterance, which can be heard only by those near at hand" ("Whisper", 2012). Doesn't this definition tell a different story? Let me change some words around. "A low, soft, sibilant voice or utterance from God which can be heard only by those near at hand." You see, the only reason it was a whisper, was because He was near and only wanted me to hear Him. God never left me. I don't know about you, but that is something I needed to know in order to move forward with my healing. God has never left you either.

"Be strong and courageous. Do not be afraid or terrified because of them, for the LORD your God goes with you; he will never leave you nor forsake you." (Deuteronomy 31:6 NIV) and "No one will be able to stand against you all the days of your life. As I was with Moses, so I will be with you; I will never leave you nor forsake you." (Joshua 1:5 NIV)

When I began to accept this and say it aloud, God allowed me to experience a very surreal moment with Him. I was laying down one night, in the depth of sorting out my feelings of hurt, and wanting to know that God never left me. I needed to know that God was there even when I didn't feel him. I needed to know that He did not cause my pain. I came to a point where I could not continue to blame God for the things that had happened to me and I needed this resolved before I could continue on to healing. I remember saying in my heart, "God, I need to know where you were when I didn't feel you or see you!"

As I laid there with my eyes closed, God took me back to pivotal moments from my past. One moment, in particular, (although there were many) when I cried myself to sleep, in pain from a deep wound I was walking through. I was begging God to stop the hurt I was feeling. Others were moments of hearing words that had pierced the core of who I am in Christ, said by people I deeply loved and cared about in my life. He took me back to those moments and specifically spoke to my heart that He never left me. I was overwhelmed with His presence, comfort and truth. I didn't realize that all I needed from Him was to know that He was there. I discovered something else along the way as well; I knew at that point that God was NOT the cause of my pain, but He was and most definitely is the healer of it.

That night I realized that the things that hurt me, hurt him because I am His child. I am his precious daughter and no Father wants his child to hurt. I believe He weeps with us when His children are inflicted with deep wounds. I finally believed from the depth of my soul that God did not cause any of this to happen, but He longs to be the healer of the damaged emotions that I had obtained from it. He did not cause your pain, but He is the healer of it. You are his child and He hurts when you hurt. He loves you!!!! He deeply loves YOU!

Journeying on to His Whisper

There is power in His whisper. A whisper can mean He is close to you and it can also mean He is speaking to you about something intimate. Hallelujah that our God is a personal God. Many times in my life, the way God whispered to me, not only showed me how close He was to me, but what He was speaking to me about was intimate. Often the reason God is whispering is not because He takes light of things or that He is not near us, but because He knows how personal the matter is.

I have spoken to women of every background you can think of while doing ministry that have been sexually and physically abused and I do not know one that experienced God loudly and abruptly shouting at her to give Him that deep dark hurt. God is an intimate God who made you. He knows the only way to respond to a wound so devastating is to approach it within the depths of your soul with His love and gentleness. "The LORD your God is in your midst, a mighty one who will save; he will rejoice over you with gladness; he will quiet you by his love; he will exult over you with loud singing." (Zephaniah 3:17 ESV) He sings songs of love over you. It is a love that has the power to quiet your heart while evident painful situations are engulfing it. I want that kind of love in my life; even if Him whispering it to me is how I can really get it in the depth of who I am. What about you? Praise God for His whisper. He is whispering not because He is far, but because sometimes an intimate soft voice is all we will hear in the middle of such pain. Don't we just sometimes need a gentle word from the Father to reassure us of His constant comfort and His presence? God knew Elijah needed to hear His whisper amidst his circumstances. He is so close. Please listen to His whisper and allow Him to meet your needs, in a still small voice that brings peace to a dreadful place.

This reminds me of a special bond I have with my nephew

when I want to get his attention from across the room. I start by calling his name and I make a very stern face that means "it's really important." He runs over to me and I come in close, cup my hands over his tiny ear and I say "I love you so much." He laughs and runs off.

I use this example because even though he heard something he has always heard out loud from me, when I make it direct, personal, and important, he loves it. It brings joy, peace, and excitement to his little world. It is our special bond, and he believes what I say to him because I made it personal. I whispered it so no one else could hear; it is meant for him and him alone.

What if that is what God wants for you and I? A phrase, we may know or have heard for years openly in church, "God loves you" or "God wants to heal you" may sound comforting in church. But when God goes out of His way to make it personal, wrap His arms around you and whispers his love for you directly to your soul, now that is something totally different. Doesn't it feel more intimate and breed a deeper trust and bond between you and God? It speaks intimacy; it meets us in a secret place no one else can be, ever. It meets us at the very depth of our being.

A woman shared her story with me about God's gentle whisper in her life. It is about a friendship betrayal, and I realize that as women this is one of the hardest things we have to overcome in our lives. I have most definitely been betrayed by a friend that I trusted deeply and I am sure you may have too. Her story will open up our eyes even more to the meaning of His whisper in our healing. Tara writes:

Starring at myself in the mirror of my downtown historic apartment, I remember thinking, something is just not right. Something about this whole relationship doesn't make any sense. Why in the world am I allowing this to go on and not do something about it?

I was standing there, tears rolling down my face, crying out to the Lord begging for an answer, begging for something, anything to help me, little did I know, the whole time God was whispering the answer so gently in my ear, but it took me a while to see that.

I went searching and when I went searching I had the help of my best friend, Sarah. Sarah knew all my desires; she knew everything about me and was ALWAYS around. We were tight and always together hanging out. She would never talk to anyone except me. I was friends with everybody and loved people, but she didn't.

Years passed by and things didn't seem right about her and people would confront me all the time about it. My best friend I met in college never had a good feeling about her, but put up with her anyways. Everyone started to get this feeling including my family. That was only the beginning.

I remember sitting in my room one night on my computer and I got a message from a guy who said his name was Chris.

I said, "Before we get this started can I ask one question?" He said, "Yes." I asked him if he believed in God.

He said, "I can't live my life without Him."

Well, from then on, we couldn't stop talking. We talked online all the time, e-mailed each other all day, it was an addiction. Chris was everything that I ever wanted. Everything about him was exactly what I had always said that I desired, he was perfect to me.

We sent pictures back and forth and I knew what he looked like and I liked it. Weeks went by and I finally asked if we could exchange phone numbers, I thought this seemed like a good idea considering we spent so much time chatting and e-mailing that it wouldn't be a big deal. He told me no! NO? Was he serious? Yes, he was.

I finally started to tell people about him. Sarah thought it was the greatest thing in the world. My other friends didn't really think so, but at that time, I didn't care. I was on top of the world, I was in love, and no one was going to put my fire out. You hear me? No one!

We spent every waking moment on the computer that we could. Now, these times, started to get out of hand. I finally started getting these mixed feelings, I wasn't sure why Chris didn't want to talk to me on the phone and I thought for a minute, he's not real, but every time I would say that, he would say no I'm just not ready.

We continued on our relationship. We had good times and bad times. I was frustrated, often, because I wanted to meet him, wanting to touch him, and I wanted to believe he existed. I thought, I go to church, I serve the Lord, and I've met the Godly man who wanted to marry me and loved me for me. I had it all together, but I was still hungry for love and so thirsty for the truth.

No matter what I got involved in, what church I went to, what Bible study I attended, I was so blinded by the junk in my life that nothing made sense to me.

I continued to talk to Chris, nothing changed. Promises were made to visit, but it never happened. Sarah kept telling me to hold it out. She thought it was a good thing and felt good about it. When I was ready to give up I would try, Chris would freak out on me and I would just keep dealing with it. He told me all the things I wanted to hear at the right time and I believed them.

Eventually I became uncomfortable around Sarah for some reason. I didn't want her around me, but I dealt with her and went on with life. Along the way, I questioned if Chris was real, I felt in my heart that I knew, but I still couldn't give it up. I was lonely before and I didn't want to be lonely again. I know the Lord was speaking to me, but I didn't want to listen. The whole time I knew the truth but I didn't want to face reality.

One Sunday I went into my room and was an emotional mess. Sarah was sitting on the end of my bed and in tears she said to me, "When it all works out, it'll be perfect for you and Chris!" I thought "Yeah right, this isn't going to work out." But for some reason those words she said to me were like nails on a chalkboard.

At this point, we were also roommates and I didn't want her in my room, on my bed, I wanted her out. I had the sickest feeling about her, and I couldn't bear to hear her voice.

Finally, one night I had enough. I was beyond aggravated. I wanted to get to the bottom of all of this and I was finally ready to face the truth. I couldn't believe what happened next. I had this obsession with Cosmopolitan online. I was online and it went straight to a story which the headline stated "Found out My Online Boyfriend was really my Best Friend." My jaw dropped. Imagine the sickest feeling you could get in your stomach, yeah that one; I felt it times a million. I read the story and it was identical to what I thought was happening to me, still not knowing if "Chris" was my "best friend" but it was like the Lord was revealing my story to me through this story.

I worked up the nerve to confront Sarah after much prayer and a very disgusting feeling. I walked into her room and confronted her, I asked her with raging tears flowing down my face if she was Chris. I asked her to be honest with me. She busted out crying and started yelling at me telling me that she couldn't believe I would even think she would do that to me, that she was my best friend and she loved me and would never hurt me in such a way.

The next day, I called a close friend of mine, and explained to her what was going on. She got on the phone and started taking care of business. She called the college Chris claimed he went to and was ready to start searching where the e-mails were coming from. She was being the best friend that Sarah was not being. Sarah just sat there while I was in this mess never once pretending like she cared.

Before I could get a call back from the friend that had been helping me, Sarah came into my room in tears and asked if she could talk to me. I KNEW it. Right then and there, I knew it. She told me she was Chris, my online boyfriend, for almost 2 years at that point. I started to open my mouth and say everything under the sun, but out of nowhere, this overwhelming peace shot throughout my whole body. The

Lord had prepared me for this moment, but I was flabbergasted. I didn't know what to say. This was a girl who claimed to be my lifelong best friend and had been for 10 years, but pulled this psychotic stunt on me. This girl was brilliant. She was extremely smart with computers and how in the world could she live two lives within one?

I couldn't wrap my head around it. She betrayed me in the WORST POSSIBLE WAY a friend could. She stabbed me in the back to say the least. She did things to me that no friend should ever think about doing. This girl wanted to control every aspect of my life, including my love life. Sarah ended up explaining to me why she did this and how she became obsessed with it and claimed she was sick and needed help.

I had been betrayed by my closest friend and had never been so hurt in my life. I ended up leaving in the middle of the night. I called my parents and spoke with my mom, and I just remember hearing her soft voice when I told her I wanted to come home, she said, "I'll be waiting." After twenty months of this ongoing mess with Chris and Sarah, I shared the whole story with my mom and she listened and never once did she say," I told you so," but she loved me and was there for me.

Every other day was a good or bad day for me. I would get very angry and upset or I would find the good in it all and smile. It took time for me to start the healing process, which is continuing. I lost all trust in people. I walked around thinking someone was watching me or following me. I felt like I had been stripped from things that I never wanted to be. I didn't understand. I started to seek God. I was going to trust Him because I knew without a shadow of a doubt that He was and will always forever be real. Days, weeks, and months passed by and there was still the good and bad days, but more good than bad.

One day God spoke to me so strongly while I was driving. I knew in order for me to really start healing I had to forgive Sarah for what she did to me. I needed to find freedom in the situation. Freedom from betrayal, heart break, dishonesty so I could be set free to start living my life the way God intended it to be. I started crying out to the Lord and I was so broken and I told the Lord that I forgave her at that very moment.

I felt a weight lifted off of my chest. I knew that day I had forgiven her and I wanted to move on with my life and just let God do healing in me.

I don't know what Sarah is doing today, but I do know that she is forgiven first and foremost by her Heavenly Father and also by me. The Bible wasn't written just for reading, it was meant for living. I cling to this verse often about my life and healing "Being confident of this, that He who began a good work in you will carry it on to completion until the day of Christ Jesus." Philippians 1:6. I pray His love abounds more and more in you and no matter how difficult the times may get for you, that you just listen to His sweet, gentle whisper.

God is whispering your name and asking you to meet Him where the wound is the deepest and the hurt is most devastating. Like Tara's story, in the midst of her confusion and hurt, she could not even begin to articulate the words God would say to her in those moments. He gave her strength to endure and make it through, but He waited in silence until the storm had passed and left its mess in every part of her life. He whispered gently to her that He loved her and was closer than she could ever imagine.

"You who are my Comforter in sorrow,
my heart is faint within me."
(Jeremiah 8:18 NIV)

God is a comforter and a source of strength. On the days you feel empty and may not even want to get out of bed, due to life's tough circumstances, He is your strength to make it through another day. Imagine this is the verse He says to you when you wake up in the morning. I love the way He whispers to us in the darkest places when we can barely lift our head to Him. He lifts our heads when we cannot.

"But you, O Lord, are a shield for me, my
glory and the One who lifts my head."
(Psalm 3:3 NKJV)

After the painful circumstance has left us stripped and bear of nothing but open wounds and sorrow, He speaks. He begins to heal us when no one else can meet us there. What if His whisper means He is closer than He has ever been and you were thinking He was the farthest He could ever be?

I would encourage you that He is closer to you than you think. God knows what this looks like for you. He knows when you start to share with Him what you've gone through that it requires vulnerability. Let Him meet you in this place of intimate details about tough matters that you have never told anyone. His whisper has the power to open, heal, free, and love you more than you can ever imagine. I don't know about you, but I am learning to love His whisper.

Chapter 4
The Death Crawl

"You, God, are awesome in your sanctuary;
the God of Israel gives power and strength
to his people. Praise be to God!"
(Psalm 68:35 NIV)

Am I crazy or do you sometimes feel like after pain has beaten you to the floor, getting up may be the hardest thing you've ever had to do? Pain takes an emotional toll and expends all of our energy, making it difficult to get up from where it left us.

I got the title of this chapter from a movie called *Facing the Giants*. I'll never forget the first time I saw this movie. The movie is about faith and facing the "spiritual" giants in your life. It involves a football team and while I'm not the biggest football fan, God used this movie to speak a truth into my life.

The coach asks one of the football players to get up and do a Death Crawl. A Death Crawl is when one player takes another teammate, more than half his weight on his back, linking elbows from the back and crawls on his hands and knees to wherever the coach gives instruction. This may seem easy for a football player, but to make it difficult the coach blind folds him. Can you imagine? As the player begins his crawl, he makes it to the 50 yard line, which is his intended destination, but the coach does not tell him. The coach continues to encourage him to keep going as if he has not reached it yet, even though he is visibly in pain and fatigued. At this point, the football player is screaming and yelling that he cannot make it. When I watch it, I literally feel the pain of pushing through in such an exhaustive, painful state.

Eventually the football player collapses in the end zone, indicating he completed 50 more yards than he was originally asked to do. He made it further than he ever expected in pure agony, drenching sweat, and desperate tears, but in the midst of his death crawl he made it when it felt impossible.

This scene brings me to tears. At first, I believe it affected me because of the beauty in the symbolism of faith. Later, I realized that I have been that football player in my walk with God. I have literally felt like the only thing I could do is crawl with half or more of my own weight on my back, blind folded, sweaty, crying, almost giving up before my end zone.

We have to make it through our death crawl. Sometimes, the baring of pain, agony, hurt, and wounds is enough to stop any of us in our tracks. We may not necessarily carry it physically on our backs, but we carry it in our spirit. This was the hardest part for me, walking by faith in God in my own healing. It may be hard for some of us to even get up and carry the load, but for many people, the most difficult task is walking by faith without being able to see what is in front of them. We don't know what is to come from all of our pain and healing and that can be hard for most of us.

I was walking in faith, believing in God for healing, but not knowing what He would reveal to me; possibly some unresolved heart issues. To go a bit deeper, I was scared that He would ask me to surrender something that I wasn't ready to give up. God was there, coaching me to the end zone even when I could not hear Him. I just had to believe that on my bad days filled with painful memories, He was still there doing work on my heart. I had to know that though I could not see, feel, or hear Him, I had to trust that His love was enough for me to make it. I had to know that my healing of this pain was not based on the stride of my death crawl, but rather it was based on the determination to get to my freedom in God. The duration of my crawl was not important. I just had to get to my healing.

The Death Crawl will determine how long it will take you to go from the 1 yard line to the end zone. God is patient, but it is important that we do not waste time. He wants us to heal and experience freedom. The first step is getting on your knees before Him; it may be difficult, but you need to begin somewhere. We started our journey with what conflicts us, caused our hearts to shatter, and how beautiful God's whisper is to us in times of pain. We must make a choice to get up and make the first step to wholeness. He's not asking you to run to the end zone, begin with getting on your knees.

Chapter 5
Buried Wounds

As I began to crawl, I realized I had buried many wounds that I had experienced in my life; whether it was a cruel comment someone said that affected me deeply, a bad dating relationship, or consequences of bad decisions I had made. We are skilled at burying what we don't want anyone to see or find out about, but it will surface in other areas of our lives. A wound can be defined as "An injury or hurt to feelings, sensibilities, reputation, etc." ("Wound", 2012).

A woman I know named Kellie was willing to share her story with me, hoping that through it you would allow God to minister to your buried wounds, as she did after realizing how they were coming up in other matters of her life.

Psalm 103:6 "The Lord executes righteousness and justice for all who are oppressed."

I'll never forget the announcement

the last day of cheerleading tryouts.. I had butterflies in my stomach. With a trembling voice, I ran up to the coach with a current cheerleader and asked her, "Did I make it?"

"No", she replied. "You didn't make the junior varsity team, but you made varsity".

I freaked out. I was excited and nervous. I proudly took my place with the big dogs my freshman year of high school.

As time progressed I started getting lots of attention from guys, especially the athletes, and being that my parents had divorced and my dad was not consistently in my life affirming me, I was eating up every bit of it. For the first time, I felt important to a male, and I liked it.

One night after a football game, some girls came over with some of the football players, including the captain of the football team, and that night at 15 years old I found myself giving up my virginity.

From there it was a downward spiral, I was watching pornography, forming internet relationships, sleeping with numerous guys, and even chasing guys down to freely give myself to them. My soul was strained; heart was aching, and my body at the disposal of whoever wanted to use it. I identified love and self-worth with this behavior. I remember looking in the mirror at one point, although I was pretty on the outside, I was screaming on the inside; for help, a way out, for my soul to be rescued.

By the time I went to college I had a list of guys that I had slept with, and sadly none of them ever loved, cared about, or had relations with me outside of sex. I had painted on several masks. I had on fear, shame, hurt, guilt, self-hatred, bitterness, anger, and deception.

The same cycle continued, I was a new face on the cheerleading squad and still very wounded and vulnerable. I began to have sexual relations with some of the athletes at college, but this time around it was different. Something began to happen in me. I was longing for the void that I was feeling to be filled.

There was a point when I would lay there, lifeless, while having sex with someone. I felt numb all over, shattered inside, and many times wondered if it would all be different if my daddy would have called to say I love you every day or to affirm who I am. I realized I hoped that temporary pleasure would fix my deep rooted pain.

In October 2003, I went home from college for fall break, and decided to turn on the television to a Christian station, which I rarely ever did. That night God met me with His love right where I was, it was real and tangible that I was lying on the floor for hours crying, because I felt Him touching those broken, wounded, shattered parts of my soul. I surrendered my lifestyle, wounds, and pain to Him that night. For the first time I had a revelation of the realness and depth of His love for me, way beyond that of an earthly father or sexual relationship.

Whether sexual impurity has led you to an unplanned pregnancy, sexually transmitted disease, broken heart, or wounded soul, God can and will heal you from the inside out. He has healed me in such a way that I have been abstinent from sex since that night in October 2003, which is now 9 years in counting. I have a clean bill of health after having a sexually transmitted disease, and look forward to one day having children. His love is so powerful, and real, once He revealed it to me on a personal level every mask began to come off one by one, and be replaced with self-respect, truth, value, freedom, faith, forgiveness, and joy.

The Lord healed me in such a way that every man that I slept with I was able to get in contact with and apologize. I asked their forgiveness for violating their body which was to be preserved for their wife within a marriage. As I released them, I was able to forgive myself.

I pray that God will reveal His love to you in such an intimate way that it will gently uproot every weed of harmful emotion that has been planted in your heart by the enemy. It will require courage, trust, and strength to look yourself in the mirror and say I'm beautiful, important, and valuable and believe it.

Your beauty is truly skin deep, and there is a love story to be written about your life with King Jesus, who is the best prince charming you could ever imagine. He keeps that promise, as I am a witness. He's still with me and longs to be with you.

Wow!! What a powerful story of God's grace, forgiveness, and love in the midst of her wounds.

The most striking sentence in this story was when she said, "I felt numb all over, shattered inside and many times wondered if it would all be different if my daddy would have called to say I love you every day or to affirm who I am." Buried wounds from fathers are deeply rooted in the depths of our souls. Our father figure in our lives is so evident and important.

Can you relate to Kellie? You may have buried wounds from a father or another male figure in your life. Have you ever wondered why women, run to sex and promiscuity when they have been inflicted by a man?

All we want in our most vulnerable moments is a man to affirm, hold, need, want, and love us. God is sufficient to fulfill all of those desires without destroying ourselves. We can have this without being promiscuous, drinking, using drugs or becoming numb to the point of total destruction. We can have a love that satisfies anything we could ever imagine. We can get through this without exposing ourselves and losing our dignity and self-worth.

I am here to tell you that there is a way that doesn't involve losing your identity in the midst of your search for love. There is a way to heal! There is a love that can overcome every wound, hurt, and injustice that has ever been imposed on you. His name is Jesus. He is more than you will ever need to conquer all that has happened to you. "Know, in all these things we are more than conquerors through him who loved us." (Romans 8:37 NIV) He is your Father. He is waiting for you to allow Him to mend your heart, so ultimately you do not resort to destruction.

Like Kellie's story, maybe it's men, sex, addiction or even suicide; I promise you that nothing is too big for God to love you through, during and after your healing. "Jesus looked at them and said, "With man this is impossible, but with God all things are possible." (Matthew 19:26 NIV) He wants to meet you in those places that you refuse to expose to anyone. He already knows you and your heart. He is waiting to carry your burdens, but you have to be willing to hand them over. Come to Him! His word says: "Come to me, all you who are weary and burdened, and I will give you rest." (Matthew 11:28 NIV)

Are you tired of running? Tired of being tired? Tired of keeping the secrets hidden only to find that they surface in other areas of your life? Are you just exhausted from carrying all of your pain? I'm sure if you relate to this story on a level of who Kellie was before she came to Christ, then you have tried everything, but Jesus. My encouragement is, try Him. He will fill that void and emptiness. What if you tried Jesus? He is waiting for you to allow Him to love you in the midst of exactly who you are right now, no masks, facades, or lies.

You Mean Me?

I am also aware that this story relates to women in the midst of walking with God. Even women who have been actively following Christ hold on to buried wounds. Though, they may not come out in a promiscuous situation or suffer from substance abuse (which they still may), they can definitely come out in other ways. For example; anger, bitterness, tempers, envy, pride and a whole bunch of other facades we use to mask the hurt deep down inside. Even though you may not think your wounds are buried; ask yourself what really causes you to lash out with behaviors that don't please God. Our enemy will fool us and he will find a way to get us to cover up anything that exposes him in our lives.

"Be alert and of sober mind. Your enemy the devil prowls around like a roaring lion looking for someone to devour." (1 Peter 5:8 NIV)

He will deceive you into believing that what you are doing that hurts others is just a "personality flaw." We need to not only take our present hurts and pains to God from our past, but we need to also continuously ask Him to search our hearts for underlying wounds that could be surfacing in our lives without us realizing it. "Search me, God, and know my heart; test me and know my anxious thoughts." (Psalm 139:23 NIV)

Let God tend to your buried wounds. We are all one mistake away from being the woman who sleeps with a man for affirmation or the woman who drinks herself to death because the pain may be greater than we think we can bear. We don't ever want to go deeper into that hole; our journey is about freedom, not about creating a deeper wound to cover up an old one.

Chapter 6
In Desperate Pursuit

I am excited about every chapter in this book, but this one is near and dear to my heart. This is a place in my own personal journey when God spoke the most intimate and clearest to me. Once I started unveiling the facade of what I was trying to be to cover up my deepest hurt, God started a fire and passion in my soul for Him. A longing only He could satisfy. This is a part of my story.

I was 15 when I realized I had hips. I remember thinking something was wrong with me and wondering why none of the other girls had hips like me. I was well endowed in my butt and hip area. I was in dance class looking at all the other girls in leotards and all I could think of was how much I hated my body. I remember thinking that I had to fix it.

At night, I would do ridiculous exercises in my bedroom before bed in hopes that it would help my figure. I was not a big girl at all, and I would never consider myself fat, but I couldn't convince myself that my shape was appealing to anyone including myself. Looking back I had a cute little figure, but no one could tell me that.

My eating disorder started with starvation also known as anorexia. It was horrible. I remember the first night I tried it. My body was aching all over and I was so weak. My best friend had stayed over that night, and I was up the whole night walking around because my body ached so badly. I needed nutrition, but I wanted a perfect body more.

Years past, and bulimia became my disorder of choice. Not the typical "throwing up what you eat disorder" (though I did that too), but I began to abuse laxatives. I took them every 4 hours around the clock; sometimes 2 at a time, every 8 hours. It was debilitating but I didn't care and I hid it well. As long as everything I ate would go straight through me, it was worth it to me, so it seemed.

I wanted to be perfect in every way. I was

a Christian, a leader in my youth group, a dancer and a fun person to be around. I was dating my first real boyfriend and all I needed was the perfect body to complete the picture. I was extremely insecure about every curve and piece of skin I could grab with my fingers that proved I was not "perfect". I became so dependent upon laxatives that by the time I wanted to stop, it was too late. I could not even have a proper bowel movement without them.

I finally broke down and told my parents. They took me to counseling, but after a few sessions I convinced them that I was fine. I continued to hide it because counseling was grueling and forced me to admit my deepest fears and insecurities of being a young woman. I didn't want to face it.

Everywhere I went I was reminded of how flawed I was. At school, in gym class, girls smaller than me would talk about how fat they were and in dance class the rest of the girls were narrow and straight as a stick from top to bottom. I filled out the bottom of our costumes graciously, and at church I would hear guys in my youth group talk about how a certain girl they liked was getting fat and she wasn't fat at all. These scenarios and conversations haunted me and I could not stop. I finally tried to stop my senior year of high school and I was successful for a little while.

My freshman year of college was approaching and with fear of gaining a "freshman 15" I was back at my old habit. I remember telling one of my best friends that I couldn't stop and right when she tried to do her friendly duty and tell me I needed help, I boldly told her not to think about stopping me.

One of my best friends that roomed with me watched me constantly run to the bathroom and take laxatives out of habit. I wanted to stop, but I couldn't, I was addicted to it I didn't even entertain her concern for me. It was selfish and inconsiderate of me and our friendship, to say the least, but I didn't care.

I took a picture with her one day and she showed it to me and I looked awful. I looked so thin and frail. I looked sick and I thought all this was to look great, what was I thinking? What had I become?

Finally, I decided the only way out was admitting I needed help, from a counselor, on my own terms. I started seeing a counselor every week at school. Counseling helped tremendously. It helped me talk out a lot of the emotions attached to the disorder. My counselor was a Christian and she helped me walk through my identity in Christ and what that looks like.

Above the effects of what it was doing to my body, it was wrecking every other area of my life as well. I couldn't function at school because I was tired. I was ill tempered because I wasn't getting proper nutrition, and I was trapped in my own prison of lies. I would allow the enemy to speak to me every time I looked in the mirror.

I walked away from bulimia that year. I struggled a little after, but God healed me. He healed me through His word and gave me the confidence in Him that I lacked in myself. I began to fight the good fight and hand over every desire to be thin and perfect to God on a daily basis. I have to say that through the years the urge has come up. It is a constant fight and it may be one I fight forever, but it is a fight I am not willing to lose. I have to be careful on certain days not to look in a mirror too much because we are all one mistake away from old habits. It is God's grace that is sufficient for me and I can do anything through Christ who gives me strength. I can fight the urge to take laxatives even when it is for a medical reason, resisting any temptation that could send me back to my destructive behavior.

I know the enemy is still after my life and identity. I still have medical issues from my disorders, but God is restoring my body every day. I am here to tell you that you are not trapped or alone. God loves, sees, and cares for you deeply. This world and the view of what women "should" look like is our worst enemy. I would encourage you to get the help you need, medically and spiritually!

I would also encourage you that besides God and counseling, what helped me most was resisting the temptation to look at magazines that talk about body image and things that took my mind there. Don't watch shows that take your mind to "why your body doesn't look like that." Take back your life and bring it before God and be desperate for His perfect love. Let Him define your identity and what you see when you *look in the mirror. Our desperation can take us many places; let it take us to the feet of Jesus.*

God wants us, all of us! Our desperation will lead us somewhere, and we must decide what our desperation will lead us to.

I was desperate for perfection; desperate for something unattainable. God healed me when nothing else would satisfy me. He healed me to the depths of my identity crisis and my need for self-worth. My worth and self-confidence is not based on a magazine, a top 100 or Sexiest Women of all Times list, it is based on a God that sees my heart.

Are We Finally on our Feet?

I was in Indiana working when I was in the middle of healing from a painful experience. My coworker and I got snowed in and work was called off for two days. Not an ideal situation for someone that was dealing with such deep hurt. We didn't have cable to distract me, but I was intrigued by a book I was reading. I don't know if it was the story necessarily, but God used the words in the book to pierce my spirit. I spent most of my time reading during the two snow days.

All I remember after completing the book was being in my room on my knees praying for God to love me past my pain.

The book did not change my life, but the God that the man talked about did. He was in a very painful situation and

I held on to every word. His pain was far worse than mine and He still believed God through one of the worst possible sorrows a person could feel. God gave me a breakthrough that weekend, it wasn't a moment probably anyone else would understand or even recognize, but it was a breakthrough for me. I finally felt like I was healing enough to stand on my feet again. This allowed me to understand that I could continue to pursue my pain and all that it holds over me; or I could start to pursue God for the deliverance of that pain. He had helped me get up and crawl to Him and finally stand again. I think, up until that point, I didn't have a desire to pursue God for the depths of my wounds and the destructive roots that were attached to them. I knew it would take time, energy, and strength I honestly did not think I had at this time in my life. He met me in my desperation. It was up to me to pursue Him. My pursuit of Him was new life to me. It showed that I was healing and I needed more of Him to not only get up, but move on with my life. When God meets us in the deep places, He meets us exactly where we are in the pain. There comes a point in our healing when we have to decide where we are going to find the rest of our restoration to wholeness.

What Are We Wearing?

At the end of that moment, I remember feeling desperate. I finally began to starve myself of self-pity. I realized that up until then I had the mentality of, "woe is me" and "why me?" Staying there is suffocating. In my pursuit to my healer, I finally decided to stop giving into one of my worst enemies during a healing journey, self-pity. Self-pity was my reasoning for many irresponsible actions. For example; bad relationships, foolish activities, and things that only poured salt on a wounded heart. I had to realize that I was not what had happened to me and I was not defined by my circumstance. Up to that point, I was both, what had happened to me and defined by my wounds. I was allowing that and I had decisions to make. I wore my wounds loudly and defined myself with my self-pity like a fresh Dolce and Gabbana suit. How many of us wear our pain like a garment that lavishes our necks? The way I wore my wounds is sickening. I had to move forward. The decision I had to make was clear.

What will I pursue in great desperation? As a woman I can admit that when I was shaken by my circumstances, I was desperate. The word desperate can seem like such an ugly word, but I started to notice something. The word was only ugly when it caused me to produce something equally ugly in my life. Desperation will push anyone to an edge, ready to jump, but what edge are we on? I used to be as bold to say that desperation was awful and no one ever wants to be there. Until I realized that the act of desperation in itself is only bad when we are pushed to the edge of something that is harmful to us and will only make us desperate for more. When your edge is God and you are desperately pushed to the edge of a life full of Him, you must pursue desperation. He is the only way out of this, even out of our self-pity parties and into our desperation for Him.

What are you desperate for? Is it the club on a Saturday night, a bar on Friday, someone to sleep with to numb your feelings, a friend that pushes you in the wrong direction, a perfect body, a drug that streams through your veins quicker than you have time to say "stop"? If we are going to continue to walk out our healing in its fullness, then we must figure out what we are desperate for. I was desperate for anything, but God. The edge I was on was sure to lead me to total destruction of the purpose God had for my life. We must take responsibility for what we have become and pursued because of our pain.

John 4:13-14 "Whoever drinks of this water will thirst again, but whoever drinks of the water that I shall give him will never thirst. But the water that I shall give him will become in him a fountain of water springing up into everlasting life." (NIV) Jesus meets a woman at a well. She had a reputation of being promiscuous. She was in self-pity of what she had become. Although physical need drew her to the well that day, she had no idea that her spiritual needs would be satiated and life would be fulfilled. She decided to go to the well alone away from all those who mocked her.

Jesus was there that day and He met her in her struggles. He offered her the water of Life so that she may never thirst again.

My question is, what well are you drawing from? Where are you going when you are thirsty and in need of something to sustain you?

Her self-pity and desperation brought her to the well. Much to her surprise, Jesus became her healer and savior that day; but she had choices to make. God wanted her all to Himself to tell her the truth about His love. With Him she will never have to thirst again.

Much like my story in Indiana, and the woman at the well, remember, self-pity turns to desperation and desperation turns to.......well the decision is yours. I can tell you that I've tried both, and if I could go back and jump right into the arms of my Savior from day one, I would do it in a heartbeat.

Desperation is never satisfied, unless satisfied by God. What you seek and pursue is what you will become. What well are you willing to drink from? One that will only make you thirst again? Or will you choose the only one that sustains you in every way? The choice is most definitely yours.

Chapter 7
Healing Into Freedom

"He has sent Me to heal the brokenhearted,
to proclaim liberty to the captives."
(Isaiah 61:1 NKJV)

This verse always does something to me. I love it! Jesus came to heal broken hearts and give liberty from those held in captivity. This is also known as freedom. This is the part of the journey when release from our wounds can begin to happen, if we allow it. We can learn to forgive others, ourselves, and heal in order to become free.

What Does Freedom Look Like?

What does freedom mean in your life? Often times, we expect freedom to be an emotion or even a feeling that we should get in a situation or circumstance at "Just the right time." I'm learning that freedom may not look like any of those things. It is a state of mind and the position of our heart. It is not only meant to be experienced, but lived. Freedom is different for everyone, but it produces life all the same.

Maybe freedom for you is being able to wake up and not wanting to hate a person that has hurt you? Perhaps it is being able to look in the mirror even once during your day and say "I'm beautiful"? Possibly it means being able to go through a day without crying because of a very painful loss? It will look different for everyone. I am sure you will know it when it begins to happen, you cannot miss it!

Another story I would like to share with you is from a woman named Erica. I asked her to share a little bit of her story with us during our journey together toward healing. Her story expresses a lot of things that she went through, but what I love about it most is she obtained freedom in the midst of it and walks it out every day of her life. Maybe you can relate to her story:

You need to lose weight. You are just like your momma- lazy, fat, and not good for anything. I swear for someone to be so smart- you sure are pretty stupid. You aren't a Christian, you're just a hypocrite. Selfish- you only think about yourself. Why are you crying, crying like a little baby?"

These are the words that haunted my childhood. My step-father would say things like this to me on a regular basis, and these were milder forms of the words. This man would become the image I had of all men for many years to come afterwards. Not only did I feel this way about men, but, God as a Father too.

I lived with my mother, and brother, and him for 7 years, ages 11 to 18. Those 7 years changed my views of men, family relationships, and myself.

I was in BETA club, National Honor Society, a member of the marching band, a lead singer in the HS chorus, top of my class, took college courses in high school, but nothing I ever did was good enough for him.

He never once attended a band or chorus concert and would begrudge days I had to be at school early because I had a club meeting. Instead of riding the bus, he or my mom would have to take me to school those days.

I was yelled at every day for something, most of the time menial things. My mom would argue with him because he yelled at me, and then I would be yelled at more because it was my fault their marriage was falling apart. No one at school ever knew that anything was wrong. I was a pro at creating a façade that my life was great.

My faith is what kept me going through

those years. I went to church on Sundays and Wednesday nights when my step dad would let me. It was there where THE Father loved me and comforted the brokenhearted.

Somehow, I still didn't get it. I felt like I needed to do things for God to love me. Be a good Christian, do good works...and that's what it was about. I was doing work for God so that He loved me, because that's what I felt I had to do for my step-dad, but I never did anything good enough for him. I could never do anything good enough for God either, but the difference was that God loved me nonetheless. I finally escaped to college when I was 18. My step-dad told me if I left, that I could never come back home. I left anyways because I felt God saying it was time to leave. I had healing to do. My freshman year was really difficult. I went to a private Christian college and was surrounded by godly influence. Only thing is, you can't hide hurt and brokenness at college. You live among your peers- you can't go home and cry.

It wasn't only my step dad who bred so much hurt and pain in my life, but my mother, after she had supported me for years, changed. I knew she was proud of me by her efforts to be there for me. When her and my step-father split up, those things stopped. And the mother I had come to know was no longer around. She began to hang out with the wrong crowd and chose a destructive lifestyle over her kids. My mother was always somewhat the stretcher of truth, but after her and my dad split, lying became a part of her new lifestyle. She lied about me, to me, and even when I caught her in lies- she continued to lie and swear what she told me was true.

I became distant from her at the beginning of her decline. God was continually healing my wounds from my step-dad and I didn't need new wounds from her. I still kept in touch with her, calling regularly more out of an obligation than of want. My mother continued to make bad choices, which in the end cost her home. Luckily, I was at college- but she and my brother were evicted. My brother came to live with me and began his own journey of healing, whereas she sunk even deeper into her madness.

During this time, she told us we had another brother that we never knew about that she gave up for adoption and then lied about his whereabouts. She later told me that she wished she would have given me and my other brother up for adoption because of the way we treated 'her.' The pain from that comment opened old wounds. I wasn't good enough and I had to earn love. I would never receive unconditional love from those who were supposed to give it to me.

However, the pain and hurt that I went through, God turned around for good. He is continually healing me from these wounds. I was able to go to college and graduate with a bachelor's degree, travel around the world, and the United States, and make some incredible friends that encourage and love me unconditionally. He has undeservedly blessed me.

Most importantly, I have found that my value was not in the words of my stepfather, the bad decisions of my mother, or the life that I grew up in. My value is given to me by my Father, God. He has made me righteous through His Son and I am fearfully and wonderfully made. He made me with a purpose, and even though I'm not fully aware of that purpose, I know it is for His glory. There are bumps in the road and times when I get discouraged, but God promises that He is always with us during the good times and bad. He has proven that over and over to me- He never leaves me, and loves me unconditionally. I pray that if you read my story and it sounds a lot like the pain you've faced, that you will find healing in God's love as well.

As hard as this story is for some of us to read and as close to home as this story hits for others, I can tell you today that Erica is finding her freedom even more every day. She is becoming free. It is not over night, but every day she takes back more of herself that got lost in the wounds that continue to come up from her childhood. Every day she has to choose freedom over the bondage from her past. Healing on the path toward freedom is not instantaneous. I wish I could tell you that Erica woke up one day and decided to get on with her life in freedom, but she didn't. Who can expect her to; who can expect us to?

I can tell you this, healing into your own freedom can look very different from someone else's. Sometimes, it takes time to admit we are bound and being held captive by rusty old chains, doesn't it? It takes time to realize we need freedom.

I would encourage you to seek God for the healing that

He is speaking to you about through His word, His Sprit, and the things in this book. Everybody's freedom looks different, don't compare yours with another's, just be in constant conversation with God as to what freedom looks like for you. In my life, I am finding that healing into freedom means to be able to experience a peace about letting go of something weighing on me. It is learning how to love people when they have hurt me. It is being reminded of a memory that used to make me angry and remembering it without emotion. It also means being able to wake up and say "Today, I am living for something bigger than myself, my situation, thoughts and ways, bigger than my deepest, most hurtful wounds and stronger than my biggest enemy." There are days when I realize that when I am not finding freedom in my life about something I have to ask myself this question: "Am I allowing myself to be held captive to the chains?" A truth that I hold dear when I talk about freedom is that God constantly reminds me that He has freed me from the chains. All I have to do is be willing to walk out of them. Freedom is not only a lifestyle and an experience, but it is a choice. Are we choosing to heal from wounds and walk away from the past? Are we choosing to forgive and allow God to change our hearts? Are we choosing freedom? The truth is God loosed the chains when He sent His son to die for us. He carried the weight of our past captivities, present, and future ones and said—you are free ...when He died in our place and rose again! John 8:36 is very clear about this....."So if the Son sets you free then you will be free indeed." (NIV)

I know that all of this takes time, but at some point we have to decide whether or not we want to live out our freedom. The first step is letting go and knowing that your chains no longer keep you captive, but you can walk out of them not because of something that you did or can do, but because of what God did and what He will DO! Healing into freedom is what the wounded desire, but we must recognize what is holding us captive and chained to our hurt and pain and make a decision to get up and walk freely! What if we stopped begging God to free us and realized He has already? Are you ready to be free?

Chapter 8
Walking In Wholeness

I have had an amazing time with you on our journey. Writing this book has been eye opening to my soul as much as I hope it has been for yours. The final part of our healing we will talk about is our wholeness in Christ and living it out daily. I left this chapter last for many reasons, but most importantly because walking out our wholeness after God has healed and freed us, is extremely important for the rest of our walk with Christ.

No matter what your situation is that you are seeking out healing for, whether it's abuse in a specific relationship or just getting the strength to face a situation that has had you bound for years. Whatever story you may relate to in this book, the one thing I don't want you to miss is that the journey will be difficult and the healing process can be long and hard, but at the end, only Christ can get you to the wholeness you deeply desire for your life. It is important that you walk out your healing to freedom and wholeness God has given you in Himself.

Dear Imprisonment....

I want to share a story with you in hopes that you too, will benefit from what God showed me in my own life of forgiving and letting go. I call it my own "Rewind Release." I am sure there are many names, even medically for this powerful scenario, but this is my name for it. I call it this because I had to come to a point where I stopped rewinding my mind back to every type of pain, hurt, and negative emotion I had memory of that had been effecting me for years. It was time to stop going back to the past in my mind and reliving every wound I had lived through. I was able to stop the broken record in my memory and release my pain and in return be free, forgive and walk whole.

Often the enemy will see that we have come this far in our journey, but he will try to paralyze us at this point. I have seen this in the lives of Christians all around me, including my own. Christians will be walking out their life and Satan deceives them into thinking they are okay, when in fact, they are still chained to the lies that keep them stuck in the same place they were even before they came to life in Christ. He paralyzes us by our thoughts and unresolved issues. He uses things that we have not fully given to God yet to hold us hostage, so much so that we will be completely freed by God, but too bound by the enemy's mental abuse to walk it out in our every day lives.

I was away on a weekend getaway, just me and the Lord and I was seeking out what was next for my life and His will for me in the upcoming year. Much to my surprise, God brought me to my knees with what He asked me to do on this trip. He spoke gently to my heart that it was time to completely free up my thoughts, my heart and my emotions that I had held onto for so long that impacted me detrimentally and would most definitely effect me in the future if I did not take care of them. I had to once and for all forgive others and forgive myself and get released from every part of my past, the things I had not yet given to Him.

At this point in my life if anyone would have asked me if I was emotionally healed by God, I would have answered them with a "Hallelujah" kind of yes; a bold yes!! I had experienced forgiveness for myself as well as granted forgiveness to others that had caused me pain. However; there are levels to healing and forgiveness. In my opinion, I believe this is one of the most important levels and the one that allows complete wholeness and restoration in our lives.

God spoke to my heart to write out every memory that I had from the very first memory of my life, I could remember, up until that moment in my life that still had a negative emotion attached to it or lack of forgiveness surrounding it. He was not suggesting that I was not healed by Him or had not experienced forgiveness in certain areas; He only wanted me to be completely freed in every area. It was time to seal the deal, if you will, in its entirety.

I wanted to think I had nothing to write, but I am here to tell you that I wrote about 10 pages of a legal pad of stuff that had been harming my thoughts, identity and heart for my entire life. Things I had known for a long time that had held me captive and finally this day was the first time I had admitted them to God.

A lot of times we think if we ignore the negative thoughts that we have about certain things then they will magically disappear, but they don't. They take power over us in some form whether we acknowledge it or not. Pain on every level must be dealt with, even the thoughts that have crept in because of bad experiences and the un-forgiveness that has rooted itself in the depth of our heart without us even noticing. The Bible is very clear about what this will do to us. "Look after each other so that none of you fails to receive the grace of God. Watch out that no poisonous root of bitterness grows up to trouble you, corrupting many." (Hebrews 12:15 NLT) The bad root not only troubles us, but corrupts us and those around us.

After I had written for a couple of hours to God about all the un-forgiveness and memories that still had a hold on me, I stood up and told God that I was finally ready to walk whole in Him. It was time to be released from my past, completely. I knew the prison I had taken up residency in within my mind. I had binding thoughts and damaged emotions. It was time to walk into wholeness in every way God had intended for me.

In response to God's direction by His Spirit, I stood at the edge of the bed and began to read everything I had written on those pages. It was hard enough to write, but to say them was a completely different level because once I said them, I was responsible for what I would do with them or what I would continue to allow them to do to me. Was I ready to completely walk in the wholeness God had for me, or was I going to leave that weekend being healed, like I had been for years and in a prison in my mind, bound to destructive thought patterns of my past?

As I spoke them out loud, God gave me instruction through speaking gently to my spirit to ask him boldly to supernaturally release me from the strings of emotions and thoughts that were attached to my heart and to those wretched memories. I asked for forgiveness I desperately needed and finally uprooted every area of un-forgiveness that had harbored in the deep, dark places of my heart for years. Not only was I released by forgiving myself that day, but so was everyone I had forgiven.

He did exactly what I had asked of Him; He supernaturally released me! I cannot explain it, but that's what makes it beautiful. I worshipped and prayed for about four hours that night in the presence of the Lord that had liberated every area of my soul. After I was done, I took all ten pages with me outside and lit them on fire and watched them burn to the ground as a symbolism that they will never have a hold on me again. To this day, I've never looked back.

People will call it what they will, but I call it God. He gave me exactly what I wanted most, peace of mind, freedom and joy. At last, I experienced true wholeness in a living God. "You will show me the path of life; in your presence is fullness of joy; at your right hand are pleasures forevermore." Psalm 16:11 (NKJV) I chose wholeness! I chose forgiveness! I want you desperately to choose the same. I want you to experience what God has designed for you to experience; true wholeness in Him.

I am not sure what your "Rewind Release" will look like, but I dare you to ask God. I dare you to be willing to walk in the wholeness He has for you.

And then there were scars.....

I heard something once, and I'll never forget it. "Scars are proof that the healing took place." I'd like to think that is what walking out our wholeness looks like. I am scarred, but if I wasn't scarred then it would still be an open wound, as many things were for me for a long time. I am learning to embrace my scars. God and I have put in some serious work, time in prayer, and many hard lessons into getting through my open wounds and I refuse to go back after they have healed, what about you? Scars are proof that God took us to a secret, intimate place with Him and whispered our name all the way to wholeness. We can not only talk about them, but we can give testimony of God's love and call Him our healer. When God healed me emotionally from all that I was wounded from, He made me whole again. He made my heart beat differently for Him and other people. Without the experiences in my life that caused me so much pain, I would never be the woman I am today in Him.

I want to share with you that as a woman on this journey with you, I have experienced heartbreak, hurt from loved ones, eating disorders, unhealthy relationships, identity crisis, hate, anger, bitterness, and other wounds that would take another book to write about. I could not describe the depth of each individual situation I had to overcome, but what I can tell you is that in order to walk in my wholeness in God I must overcome evil with good.

"Do not be overcome by evil,
but overcome evil with good."
(Romans 12:21 NIV)

I must overcome the things the enemy meant for my destruction and allow God to grow me deeper and stronger with His goodness. I want to tell you how to admit, forgive, heal, walk freely, and become whole after all of your wounds, but I cannot. God must do this. Your wholeness is based on your will to bring yourself to the healer so that He can provide you with the love and strength you need to fight and overcome the hurt that is inside of you. He will help you overcome, but you must seek His face daily, by the seconds, minutes and hours of your day. "Look to the LORD and his strength; seek his face always." (Psalm 105:4 NIV) Wholeness allows you to become confident in your healer so that you can liberate others around you to obtain healing and wholeness as well in that same healer.

I Am Redeemed!!!!

Allow Him to take you back to every moment that hurt you like He did me. Allow Him to not only be your healer, but your redeemer. *Redeem*: "To make good or fulfill, to set free, as from captivity; rescue; ransom." (Macmillan, 1981) This definition is full of truth that God desires for you and your life. He wants to make things good, set you free and rescue you entirely. He can redeem with His love and teach you to forgive others and love yourself. Allow Him to redeem the child in you that was taken advantage of, the teenager that was lost in suicide, doubts of self-worth, or the adult that cannot seem to forgive because of all the pain you have endured over the years. I'm not saying you will forget these moments, but when you do remember these moments they will be a testimony of where God has brought you by His love and grace and will no longer be a source of great pain. You will actually be able to utter the words of your situation without falling apart and give a testament of God's faithfulness to those who trust in Him. You will be healed!! Let God love you through the memory and redeem all that you lost in your painful experiences. Remember that He never left you and desires to redeem your heart. He is a REDEEMER of life....Job talks about this extensively in Job 19.

"My relatives have failed me, my close
friends have forgotten me....."
(NKJV)

And he goes on to say in the same chapter...

"For I know my Redeemer lives, and at the
last He will stand upon the earth."
(NKJV)

When everyone has walked away that should have stayed, He remains and His love sustains you through it all. God was silent in Job's worst pain for 37 chapters and He still recognized Him as the redeemer.

Allow God to free you from the moments that you allowed to have power over your heart and life for so long.

This healing journey for you and your life in Christ is of upmost importance for you. Healing from all the hurt in your life presently or in the past allows you to live a more fulfilled life. You leave room for deeper love for others and yourself, stronger faith in God, and a love for Christ that you could only know through such an intimate walk with Him. Let our journey together produce wholeness that can only be obtained by God, who takes the time to remind us of how much He loves us and desires our heart. Your soul is where you and God dwell, the silent places of your being that can only be reached by Him. Keep this intimacy you have experienced through this journey. Give God everything. Walk in pure wholeness only healing in God can breed.

A Prayer for My Readers

I wanted to take a moment to share a prayer with you. God's desire for you is to heal from every wound you have ever experienced. Let's pray for God to open our hearts and point out the things that we must give to Him in order to move on with our life in total freedom.

God,

I come to you today bare, stripped of anything I have left to give to this woman from my own heart, as my heart is open and wounds exposed as well. I pray for the woman reading this book, or maybe even just this prayer. I pray for the wounds she carries and has buried so deep no matter what that looks like to her to come up and be dealt with.

You speak freedom over her life. Whatever wound she is coming to you with, I pray over her pain and hurt that your freedom would fall on her life. I pray that she would find forgiveness for the person who has hurt her or inflicted her with any level of pain that has now resulted in a wound that she must allow you to heal. If that wound is rape from a man she barely knew, a molestation from a pastor or anyone that should never have put their hands on her as your daughter. If the wound is the innocence that was taken from her when she was growing up, every adult that never said enough to her or never said a word and pushed her pain under the rug for a little girl only to deal with as an adult, help her walk this out hand in hand with you. I pray for healing for her precious soul from physical, sexual, and/or verbal abuse that has caused her, as your daughter, to think of herself any different than you had created her to think about herself. I pray your love would overwhelm her in the midst of her deepest pain.

Comfort the woman reading this who was or is suicidal or had an eating disorder and set her free. For the woman that is suffering the loss of someone they deeply loved, whether by death, divorce or any type of separation that wounds deeply, sustain her and fill that emptiness with your love.

I pray for the breaking of chains the enemy has this woman bound to. If this woman has suffered through an affair or a painful divorce, Lord give her your peace in the secret place of her soul that only you can give. Father, wrap your arms around her as she pours out her heart to you. Redeem her from the pain that has stolen many thoughts, moments, childhood memories, adulthood occasions and numerous nights of crying out when no one heard. Redeem every part of her life that has been affected by her pain and has caused her to pursue sex, men, drugs, or alcohol as a numbing to what she has deep down inside.

God, I pray that she would have the strength to fight the temptation and the pull to promiscuity the enemy often has on us as women during our painful moments. Deliver this woman from any terrible relationships, friendships or any relationships that are desperately damaging to the plan You have for her life. She needs your love, healing, grace, and tender care, she needs you! I can do nothing for her besides lead her to you. I bring this woman, with every wound possible, with every ounce of my being to you and I lay her at your feet.

Work in her heart and heal her from the inside out. Show

her who you are and what she is meant to be in you. Remind her that she is only strong in you and to get through all of this without you would be an endless cycle. In the midst of her lonely, cold, hard nights, whisper in her ear who you are and how much she means to you and your endless love for her.

You are the vine, and she must be connected to you in order to produce good fruit; fruit that pleases you. As you uncover these deep wounds in her heart, be tender and careful as you always are and remind her that complete vulnerability to you is complete freedom in her.

Give her the power to forgive those who have hurt her so deeply and then forgive herself for holding on to hurt so tightly that it has produced hatred, bitterness and anger in her life. Help this woman to make a choice that she will not become one who wounds others because she has been wounded. That is only an endless circle of pain for many generations.

Father, help her to break the generational cycle of hurt and pain that has been inflicted on the ones she loves the most from the direct effect of pain she has experienced herself. Let her know the importance of giving you every intricate detail of her pain and the circumstance that has brought her directly to you for healing.

Meet this precious woman exactly where she is today and reveal to her who You say that she is. Remind her that she is not what has happened to her and she is not defined by the circumstances she is in. You lift her head and you walk with her. Show her that she is never alone, even in the midst of all the pain she has and all the pain she has buried year after year. Reveal to her that wounds untouched, buried and not dealt with will only breed bitterness, anger and will be her only source of emotion that drives her daily. You have made her to live daily with you and without allowing you to tend to her at the measures necessary she is abandoning every part of herself that you have created her to be complete in you.

God, you are a good God and even more intimately you are an amazing father, redeemer and healer. You are everything that the woman reading this book needs if she will only let you permeate every part of her being that no one else is allowed to; the places where only her and her pain have dwelled. This woman has a new beginning in You and no matter what she has done; you are ready and willing to set her feet on a new path ready, running in righteousness straight to you. All it takes is an open heart for you to begin the amazing work in her that you have so desired for her.

God, let her be assured that you never left her, in any moment, in any situation.

I lay this woman at your feet. Mend her broken heart; carry her heavy burdens and most of all heal and redeem all that has been taken from her because of this pain she is in.

God RESTORE the daughter she has and always will be to you. God call her to you and embrace her like never before.

In Jesus Name!! Amen!!

References and Resources

Whisper. (2012). *Dictionary.com.* Retrieved from
    http://dictionary.reference.com/

Wound. (2012). *Dictionary.com.* Retrieved from
    http://dictionary.reference.com/

Macmillan. (1981). Dictionary for Students. New York:
Macmillan Publishing Company.

Author Bio

Brittney Perillo lives with husband Richard in Buffalo, New York. They call The Chapel in Getzville, NY their church home. Brittney has been blessed with several ministry opportunities to speak, teach and lead in the following settings and capacity: Abstinence Programs, Inner City Youth Programs, Young Women's Conferences, Bible studies, Buffalo City Schools, and Youth Camps. She is currently enrolled at Liberty University where she will earn a degree in Religion, she will also obtain a minor in Christian Counseling. In her free time Brittney enjoys blogging, journaling and reading.

CPSIA information can be obtained at www.ICGtesting.com
Printed in the USA
BVOW021859121212

308070BV00001B/5/P